REVOLUTIONARY LESSONS ROOTED IN

NEVER LEAD ALONE WORKBOOK

Foundational Ideas for Growth from Keith Ferrazzi's Book.

GOLDENQUILL PRESS

CONTENTS

CHAPTER 1: EMBRACING CO-ELEVATION

Key Insights:

- Co-elevation is the commitment of each team member to uplift and push one another toward shared goals.

- It emphasizes a symbiotic relationship where success is mutual and dependent on collective efforts.

- By fostering an environment of mutual support, teams can achieve higher productivity and more innovative solutions.

- Co-elevation relies on open communication, respect, and a genuine interest in the personal and professional growth of fellow teammates.

- This approach challenges traditional hierarchical structures by distributing leadership and responsibilities, creating a more dynamic and flexible working environment.

Reflection Questions:

Reflect on a time when mutual support within a team led to a great outcome. What behaviors made this possible?

_____

_____

_____

_____

_____

_____

_____

_____

_____

How can the principles of co-elevation change the way you currently engage with your colleagues?

_____

_____

_____

_____

_____

_____

_____

_____

_____

What barriers to co-elevation exist in your current team or organizational culture?

_____

_____

_____

_____

_____

_____

_____

_____

_____

_____

How might you personally contribute to a culture of co-elevation in your workplace or community?

_____

_____

_____

_____

_____

_____

_____

_____

_____

_____

What would be the impact on team performance if every member adopted a co-elevation mindset?

_____

_____

_____

_____

_____

_____

_____

_____

_____

Actionable Steps:

1. Start each meeting by acknowledging a positive contribution from each team member, reinforcing the practice of mutual appreciation and support.

2. Organize regular team-building activities that are not just fun but also include sessions on sharing skills and knowledge among team members.

3. Implement a 'co-elevation hour' each week where team members can discuss challenges and seek advice from the group, fostering a collaborative problem-solving environment.

"Alone we can do so little; together we can do so much." — Helen Keller

CHAPTER 2: ESTABLISHING PEER-TO-PEER ACCOUNTABILITY

Key Insights:

- Peer-to-peer accountability involves team members holding each other responsible for meeting team goals and standards without solely relying on hierarchical oversight.

- This form of accountability promotes a sense of ownership and responsibility among team members, enhancing the commitment to collective success.

- Effective peer accountability requires clear communication of expectations and roles within the team.

- It fosters a culture of transparency where feedback is exchanged constructively and regularly to facilitate improvement and address issues promptly.

- Building a system of peer-to-peer accountability can lead to a more empowered and engaged workforce, reducing the burden on leaders and enhancing team dynamics.

Reflection Questions:

How do you react when a colleague holds you accountable? Consider both positive and negative experiences.

_____

_____

_____

_____

_____

_____

_____

_____

What methods can you use to more effectively communicate your expectations to your peers?

In what ways can you improve the way you provide feedback to ensure it is constructive and not critical?

_____

_____

_____

_____

_____

_____

_____

_____

How can your team create a safe space for
accountability where members do not feel threatened
or defensive?

_____

_____

_____

_____

_____

_____

_____

_____

_____

_____

What are the potential challenges of implementing peer-to-peer accountability in your team, and how can these be overcome?

_____

_____

_____

_____

_____

_____

_____

_____

Actionable Steps:

1. Establish regular peer review sessions where team members can discuss their progress and challenges related to their tasks.

2. Develop a peer recognition program that allows team members to acknowledge each other's contributions and successes, reinforcing positive behaviors and outcomes.

3. Create a clear and concise document outlining team roles, responsibilities, and the process for holding each other accountable, ensuring everyone understands what is expected of them.

"Accountability is the glue that ties commitment to the result." — Bob Proctor

CHAPTER 3: BUILDING PERSONAL TRUST WITHIN THE TEAM

Key Insights:

- Personal trust within a team is foundational to creating a secure, open environment where members feel confident to share ideas and challenges without fear of judgment or retribution.

- Trust is built through consistent actions, honesty, and integrity, showing team members they can rely on one another.

- A high-trust environment enhances collaboration and speeds up decision-making processes because team members are confident in each other's abilities and intentions.

- Developing personal trust requires vulnerability from all team members, meaning they must be willing to share their weaknesses and mistakes as well as successes.

- Regular, open communication and the celebration of team achievements play a significant role in strengthening trust.

Reflection Questions:

Reflect on a past team experience where trust was either strongly present or noticeably lacking. How did this affect the team's performance?

_____

_____

_____

_____

_____

_____

_____

_____

_____

What actions can you take to demonstrate reliability and build trust with your team members?

_____

_____

_____

_____

_____

_____

_____

_____

_____

How can leaders foster an environment that encourages vulnerability and open communication?

_____

_____

_____

_____

_____

_____

_____

_____

_____

_____

What strategies can be implemented to repair trust in a team where it has been damaged?

_____

_____

_____

_____

_____

_____

_____

_____

_____

_____

Consider your current team dynamics. What specific

barriers to trust exist, and how can they be addressed?

_____

_____

_____

_____

_____

_____

_____

_____

_____

Actionable Steps:

1. Initiate team-building exercises that focus not just on productivity but also on personal interactions and sharing personal stories, helping members connect on a deeper level.

2. Implement a "no-blame" approach to mistakes and focus on solutions and learning opportunities to strengthen trust in handling errors and setbacks.

3. Schedule regular one-on-one meetings between team members and leaders to discuss career goals, personal challenges, and feedback, thereby enhancing transparency and trust.

"Trust is built when someone is vulnerable and not taken advantage of." — Bob Vanourek

CHAPTER 4: IMPLEMENTING SHARED FEEDBACK MECHANISMS

Key Insights:

- Shared feedback mechanisms are crucial for continuous improvement and fostering a culture of open communication and growth within a team.

- Effective feedback is specific, timely, and focused on behaviors rather than personal attributes, facilitating constructive discussions and personal development.

- Implementing regular, structured feedback sessions helps normalize the practice and reduces anxiety associated with receiving feedback.

- Encouraging a bidirectional feedback flow—where team members feel comfortable giving and receiving feedback from peers and leaders alike—strengthens team dynamics and trust.

- Automating part of the feedback process through tools can ensure consistency and regularity, but personal touchpoints remain essential for meaningful interactions.

Reflection Questions:

Think about the most helpful feedback you have ever received. What made it stand out, and how did it influence your behavior or decisions?

_____

_____

_____

_____

_____

_____

_____

How comfortable do you feel giving feedback to others? What factors influence your comfort level?

What are some challenges your team faces in implementing effective feedback mechanisms, and how can they be overcome?

_____

_____

_____

_____

_____

_____

_____

How can leaders ensure that feedback mechanisms are

inclusive and consider the diverse perspectives within

a team?

_____

_____

_____

_____

_____

_____

_____

_____

_____

_____

What role do empathy and emotional intelligence play

in the effectiveness of feedback mechanisms?

_____

_____

_____

_____

_____

_____

_____

_____

Actionable Steps:

1. Develop a feedback charter that outlines how feedback should be given and received, emphasizing respect, specificity, and a focus on growth.

2. Train all team members on effective communication techniques and emotional intelligence to enhance the quality and reception of feedback.

3. Establish regular feedback cycles, such as monthly or quarterly reviews, complemented by real-time feedback to address immediate issues or praise accomplishments.

"Feedback is the breakfast of champions." —

Ken Blanchard

CHAPTER 5: DEVELOPING TEAM RESILIENCE

Key Insights:

- Team resilience refers to the ability of a group to endure stress, adapt to challenges, and recover quickly from setbacks to continue performing effectively.

- Building resilience within a team involves fostering a supportive environment where members feel secure in facing difficulties together.

- Resilient teams are characterized by strong communication, mutual trust, and a shared belief in their collective strength and capabilities.

- Encouraging problem-solving skills, flexibility, and adaptability among team members is crucial for developing resilience.

- Learning from past experiences and failures, rather than dwelling on them, helps teams strengthen their ability to handle future challenges.

Reflection Questions:

Reflect on a challenge your team has faced. How did the team respond, and what learning came from that experience?

_____

_____

_____

_____

_____

_____

_____

_____

What qualities do you think are essential for resilience in a team setting? How do these qualities manifest in day-to-day interactions?

How can leaders nurture an environment that
promotes resilience and encourages teams to embrace
challenges as opportunities?

_____

_____

_____

_____

_____

_____

_____

What strategies can be implemented to better prepare
your team for unexpected setbacks?

_____

_____

_____

_____

_____

_____

_____

_____

_____

_____

How does fostering individual resilience contribute to
the overall resilience of the team?

_____

_____

_____

_____

_____

_____

_____

_____

_____

Actionable Steps:

1. Implement regular resilience training and workshops that focus on skills like stress management, adaptive thinking, and effective communication.

2. Create a "resilience resource" of tools and techniques that team members can access during challenging times to help manage their responses and emotions.

3. Encourage and facilitate open discussions about failures and mistakes as learning opportunities, thereby reducing stigma and promoting a growth mindset.

"The oak fought the wind and was broken, the willow bent when it must and survived." — Robert Jordan

CHAPTER 6: ADOPTING AGILE WAYS OF WORKING

Key Insights:

- Agile methodologies prioritize flexibility, continuous improvement, and rapid response to change over rigid planning and hierarchical decision-making.

- Adopting agile ways of working encourages a culture where teams can experiment, learn from outcomes, and adjust processes quickly to enhance efficiency and effectiveness.

- Agile teams break work into smaller, manageable units, allowing for frequent reassessment and adaptation of goals and strategies based on real-time feedback and changes in circumstances.

- This approach promotes collaboration across functions and levels, involving team members in decision-making processes and empowering them to take ownership of outcomes.

- Key to agile success is maintaining clear communication, frequent updates, and the iterative delivery of work products, ensuring all team members are aligned and can contribute effectively.

Reflection Questions:

Consider your current work processes. How could they be improved by integrating agile methodologies?

_____

_____

_____

_____

_____

_____

_____

_____

What reservations might you or your team have about transitioning to agile ways of working? How can these be addressed?

_____

_____

_____

_____

_____

_____

_____

_____

_____

How does the concept of 'failing fast' align with your team's current approach to projects and innovation?

_____

_____

_____

_____

_____

_____

_____

_____

_____

_____

What steps can be taken to foster a more collaborative
and cross-functional team environment that supports
agile principles?

_____

_____

_____

_____

_____

_____

_____

_____

_____

_____

How can leaders ensure that agile methodologies are
consistently applied and that the team remains flexible
and responsive to change?

_____

_____

_____

_____

_____

_____

_____

_____

Actionable Steps:

1. Begin implementing agile methodologies by starting with small pilot projects to familiarize the team with agile practices and gain buy-in through visible successes.

2. Establish daily stand-up meetings to enhance communication and update team members on project progress, challenges, and shifts in priorities.

3. Train team members on agile tools and techniques, such as Scrum or Kanban, to ensure everyone understands and can effectively contribute to the new processes.

"Flexibility is the key to stability." — *John Wooden*

CHAPTER 7: CREATING A HIGH-PERFORMANCE SOCIAL CONTRACT

Key Insights:

- A high-performance social contract is an agreement among team members that outlines expected behaviors, communication norms, and mutual commitments to foster a productive and respectful work environment.

- Establishing such a contract promotes clarity and alignment on team values, roles, responsibilities, and the methods for addressing conflicts and challenges.

- This contract serves as a foundation for building trust and accountability, crucial elements in achieving and maintaining high team performance.

- Effective social contracts are collaboratively developed to ensure buy-in from all team members, reflecting their input and addressing their concerns.

- Regular reviews and updates of the social contract are necessary to adapt to evolving team dynamics and organizational goals.

Reflection Questions:

What values are most important to you and your team, and how can they be incorporated into a social contract?

_____

_____

_____

_____

_____

_____

_____

_____

_____

How can a social contract help in managing conflicts within your team?

_____

_____

_____

_____

_____

_____

_____

_____

_____

What mechanisms can be included in the social contract to ensure ongoing communication and feedback among team members?

_____

_____

_____

_____

_____

_____

_____

_____

_____

_____

How often should the social contract be revisited and

revised, and who should be involved in this process?

_____

_____

_____

_____

_____

_____

What are some potential challenges in implementing a
social contract, and how can they be mitigated?

Actionable Steps:

1. Organize a team workshop to collaboratively draft the initial social contract, ensuring all team members can contribute their ideas and expectations.

2. Integrate a regular review session, perhaps bi-annually or annually, into your team's schedule to assess the relevance and effectiveness of the social contract and make necessary adjustments.

3. Establish clear protocols within the social contract for conflict resolution and ensure these are understood and accessible to all team members to foster a cooperative and supportive work environment.

"Coming together is a beginning, staying together is progress, and working together is success." — Henry Ford

• • •

CHAPTER 8: LEVERAGING COLLABORATIVE TECHNOLOGY AND AI

Key Insights:

- Incorporating collaborative technology and artificial intelligence (AI) can significantly enhance team efficiency, communication, and decision-making capabilities.

- These technologies facilitate real-time data sharing, streamlined workflows, and automated routine tasks, allowing team members to focus on more strategic activities.

- AI tools can provide predictive insights, risk assessments, and personalized recommendations, helping teams anticipate challenges and optimize their responses.

- Collaborative platforms enable seamless integration of various functions within an organization, ensuring all team members are on the same page and reducing silos.

- It's important to choose technologies that are scalable and can adapt to the team's growing and changing needs.

Reflection Questions:

What are the current technological tools your team uses, and how effectively do they support your team's work?

What potential barriers might your team face in integrating new collaborative technologies and AI, and how can these be overcome?

_____

_____

_____

_____

_____

_____

_____

_____

_____

How can AI be used to predict and solve challenges within your team's projects?

_____

_____

_____

_____

_____

_____

_____

_____

_____

In what ways can real-time data sharing impact your team's performance and decision-making processes?

_____

_____

_____

_____

_____

_____

_____

_____

_____

What training or resources are needed to ensure all team members can effectively use the new technologies?

_____

_____

_____

_____

_____

_____

_____

_____

_____

Actionable Steps:

1. Conduct a needs assessment to identify gaps in current technology use and determine which collaborative tools and AI solutions could fill those needs.

2. Implement training sessions for all team members to ensure they are proficient in using new technologies and understand how to leverage AI tools for maximum benefit.

3. Establish a feedback loop where team members can regularly evaluate the technology's impact and suggest improvements or changes to better meet their needs.

"The new electronic interdependence recreates the world in the image of a global village." — Marshall McLuhan

CHAPTER 9: CULTIVATING AN INCLUSIVE AND INNOVATIVE TEAM CULTURE

Key Insights:

- An inclusive and innovative team culture is vital for attracting and retaining diverse talent, driving creativity, and enhancing problem-solving capabilities across the organization.

- Inclusivity involves recognizing and valuing the unique contributions of each team member, promoting an environment where everyone feels respected and heard.

- Innovation thrives in a culture that encourages risk-taking, experimentation, and learning from failure, without fear of negative repercussions.

- Cultivating such a culture requires active and continuous efforts from leadership to model inclusivity and support innovative practices.

- Regular training and development opportunities focused on diversity, equity, and inclusion can help embed these values into the team's everyday interactions.

Reflection Questions:

How diverse is your team in terms of backgrounds, perspectives, and skills, and how does this diversity enhance the team's performance?

_____

_____

_____

_____

_____

_____

_____

_____

_____

What practices are currently in place to ensure all team members feel included and valued?

_____

_____

_____

_____

_____

_____

_____

_____

_____

_____

Can you identify any barriers to innovation within your team? How might these be addressed to foster a more creative environment?

_____

_____

_____

• • •

_____

_____

_____

_____

_____

_____

_____

What steps can leaders take to more actively promote
and reward risk-taking and innovation?

_____

_____

_____

_____

_____

_____

_____

How can regular feedback and open communication channels enhance inclusivity and innovation within the team?

Actionable Steps:

1. Implement a structured mentorship program that pairs team members from different backgrounds to promote knowledge sharing and mutual understanding.

2. Schedule regular 'innovation challenges' or hackathons to encourage creative thinking and problem-solving in a fun, collaborative setting.

3. Develop a recognition system that rewards not only successful innovations but also the learning derived from unsuccessful experiments.

"Diversity is being invited to the party; inclusion is being asked to dance." — Verna Myers

CHAPTER 10: SUSTAINING TEAMSHIP FOR LONG-TERM SUCCESS

Key Insights:

- Sustaining teamship requires ongoing effort to maintain the team dynamics that lead to high performance, innovation, and inclusivity over the long term.

- Continual investment in team development, through training, shared experiences, and reinforcing a positive team culture, is essential to keep the momentum of teamship.

- Regular reassessment of team goals, roles, and processes ensures that the team remains aligned with changing organizational objectives and external environments.

- Effective leadership plays a crucial role in modeling behaviors and values that sustain teamship, such as transparency, accountability, and mutual support.

- Building resilience and flexibility into the team's operations can help them adapt to changes and challenges without losing their core strengths.

Reflection Questions:

What long-term strategies can be implemented to ensure continuous development and engagement of team members?

_____

_____

_____

_____

_____

_____

_____

_____

_____

How can the team's achievements and progress be regularly evaluated and celebrated to maintain motivation and commitment?

What role do leaders play in ensuring the sustainability of teamship, and how can they be supported in this role?

_____

_____

_____

_____

_____

_____

_____

_____

_____

How can the team adapt to external changes while maintaining the core values and practices that define their teamship?

_____

_____

_____

_____

_____

_____

_____

_____

_____

_____

In what ways can team members be empowered to take a proactive role in sustaining teamship?

_____

_____

_____

_____

_____

_____

_____

_____

Actionable Steps:

1. Establish a 'teamship audit' every six months to evaluate how well the team is adhering to the principles of teamship and identify areas for improvement.

2. Create a 'team charter' that evolves as the team grows and changes, keeping everyone aligned on what teamship means and how it should be practiced.

3. Encourage a culture of continuous learning by providing regular opportunities for team members to acquire new skills and share knowledge within the team.

"Great teams do not hold back with one another. They are unafraid to air their dirty laundry. They admit their mistakes, their weaknesses, and their concerns without fear of reprisal." — Patrick Lencioni

FINAL SELF-EVALUATION
QUESTIONS

Reflect on how your understanding of teamship has evolved after completing this workbook. What key changes will you implement in your team based on this new understanding?

_____

_____

_____

_____

_____

_____

_____

_____

How effectively do you feel you can apply the principles of co-elevation in your current team environment? What steps will you take to improve this?

_____

_____

_____

_____

_____

_____

_____

_____

In what ways have you contributed to building or hindering trust within your team? Outline a plan to enhance trust based on insights from the workbook.

• • •

_____

_____

_____

_____

_____

_____

_____

_____

_____

_____

Evaluate how the introduction of agile methodologies could impact your team's performance. What are the potential challenges and benefits?

_____

_____

_____

_____

_____

_____

_____

_____

_____

_____

Considering the concepts of peer-to-peer accountability and feedback mechanisms, how prepared do you feel to lead these initiatives? What resources or support might you need?

_____

_____

_____

_____

_____

How can you personally foster an inclusive and innovative culture within your team? Identify specific actions you can take to promote these values.

_____

_____

Assess the role of collaborative technology in your team's current operations. How might you enhance or modify this to improve teamship?

_____

_____

_____

_____

_____

_____

_____

_____

_____

Reflect on how you have dealt with team challenges and conflicts in the past. Based on the workbook, what new strategies would you use in future situations?

_____

_____

_____

_____

_____

_____

_____

_____

_____

_____

How does the concept of a high-performance social contract appeal to you? Draft an outline of what your ideal social contract would include.

• • •

_____

_____

_____

_____

_____

_____

_____

_____

_____

Looking ahead, how will you measure the success of the teamship principles implemented in your team? What metrics or indicators will be most important?

_____

_____

_____

Made in the USA
Las Vegas, NV
14 December 2024

14166166R00046